Poems t Enlighten the Mind

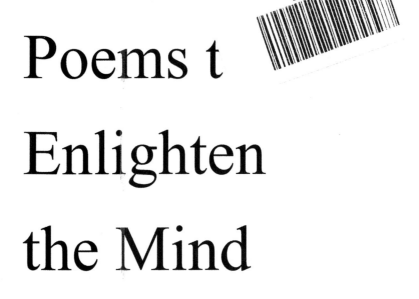

By George Majcherczyk-Olczak

To my brother Mark,
who inspired me to write
this book.

Contents:

Foreword

This collection of poems is quite unlike my own, however its' unique style of writing is engaging and enraptures the reader's imagination as they imagine themselves immersed in between the lines of this dense, intricately designed poetry. George's use of phrasing and stability allows him to communicate to the reader in a special way, and I hope you reading his works in this compilation will help you see this. I also hope that you are inspired to write your own poetry because of this book and saving the best till last: ENJOY!

Mark Majcherczyk-Olczak,
Poet and Literacy Expert

Light

The careful flickering that
brings warmth,
Softly dancing in the cold
night.
It can be a flame yet a spark
of hope and joy,
To aid in prayer and light the
way
To show the path of
righteousness
And display its bright array
To be a light
To lighten the world
To bring comfort
To enlighten our lives.

Rain

Gush down you droplets of
misery,
Pouring yourself onto the
land
Bringing panic and distress
Once the situation worsens,
Why can't you simmer
down?
Take a break?
Well, you are needed for
plants to grow
And you bring new life
So we just have to live with
you

London buses

Red buses frantically
swimming down each road,
Smothering their colors onto
the busy streets.
On their sides are
advertisements,
Hoping to catch the eye of
the fellow pedestrian
As the hobble across the
pavement,
They are unique and famous
So hop on board and absorb
the magic of London.

Football

Ambitious chanting fills the
air
As fans stream in through the
turnstiles
The hustle and bustle
continues,
Fans find their seats with a
beer in hand
And the anthems are
patriotically sung
Then with the first kick of the
ball
Everyone admires the scenes,
These are the wonders of the
beautiful game.

Cricket

He's come into bowl and oh… wait
a minute…
Out! LBW! The batsman instantly
reviews it!
DRS has come into play and let's
look at this again,
Pitching outside, impact off,
wickets missing.
Not out. The batsman ecstatic,
pumping his fists
since he had the chance to win the
match for his team.
One ball, one run… Rapidly
beating, his heart pumped faster
than ever, he swung his bat
performed the action of a reverse
scoop, and gazed in awe as the ball
went for six! His standing ovation
was one to be remembered.

Tennis

Ace.Ace.Ace. The match started to turn into a demolition job, as he got point after point.
Smiling remarkably, he watched as the crowd gave him rapturous applause.
Inhaling deeply, he raised his racket, threw the ball up into the air, and struck it cleanly.
Carefully, he watched as it was placed perfectly into the box, his opponent slipped on the clay-he won.
He won. Finally, the trophy was his-he lifted it up high and thanked everyone!

Winter

Silently, the thick blanket of
frost covered the surroundings,
Creating a sight to behold.
 The chill of the winter air
snapped a bite into the last
pockets of relatively warm air,
making it feel colder than ever.
Ah.Ah.Ah. The soft sound of
cold breath in the winter's morn
Brought a reminder that
Christmas was around the
corner
Bringing many a merry and
tidings of gladness,
Filling their hearts with warmth
and excitement
Awaiting the joy of Christmas!

Spring

Fluttering angelically, the
birds vocalized away,
Their sweet music resonating
in the crisp air.
Flowers abloom, springing
new life,
 Springtime upon us, the
gentle warmth is embraced
With much gratitude, as the
cold of winter is banished.
Oh! How wonderful a sight
nature brings,
The grandeur of spring really
uplifts the soul
And brings tidings of warmth
and joy.

Summer

Trickling down her face, the
sweat visibly bothered her.
Her face was caked with
thick, greasy sweat.
Frustratingly, she turned to
the sun and waved her fists,
This nightmare heat was
absolutely unbearable-
I pray ye, lower the
temperature! No answer.
However, knowing that
Autumn was in a few
months,
She positively put up with the
heat by relaxing in the pool.

Autumn

A wash of brown and orange
covered the streets.
Leaf after leaf fell down from
the branches,
Causing a hazard of slippery
streets.
The deafening of the leaf
blowers caused aggravation,
however, the streets were
cleared and there was no hazard
Any more.
Until… More leaves came
thudding down, and the
Familiar mix of brown and
orange was clearly visible once
more, and so the leaf blowers
sounded their trumpets in return.

Anxiety

Eyes twitching, fingers
fidgeting, the nerves settled in…
The churning of the stomach
only added to the internal
Nightmare that was being
experienced.
The dreadful feeling of panic
and unproven responsibility
Consumed the very heart and
soul that formed the person.
Oh no! What if I make a
mistake? Will others judge me?
The thoughts of the
consequences were terrifying,
Anything could happen. Failure.
Success.

Confidence

Wait. It's that feeling again.
The positive blood flow that
strengthens your heart and
Increases your inner peace.
Confidence.
The power of confidence is
unmatched.
It can completely transform
you as a person,
Improve your life, strengthen
your day to day
Encounters.
It makes you special.
You stand out.
So be confident, and be
proud!

Books

Indulging passionately in a
stunning read,
Teleporting you to other places,
different experiences,
Other people.
Books are a powerful tool.
They aid us in entertainment, relief,
and most importantly,
They provide us with an escape
from the real world.
Books are a wonderful tool.
We can delve into the depths of
knowledge and fantasy in a book,
and pretend to be different people,
experience other people's lives,
dream, relive our childhoods.
Books are a magical tool.

Thunder

Strike! Strike! Oh, you destructive tyrant!
The immense power wielded is capable of causing mass dilapidation and social chaos.
Ominously, its soft grumble frightens a fair few,
causing panic and in some cases extreme anxiety.
In the dead of night, the occasional clap of thunder can really startle people and catch them off guard.
It's actually quite amusing how some thunder can scare people.
Some might bury themselves under their blankets, and others might clamp their ears tight shut; but in the end, it's just nature, and the world we live in.

Loss

Frantically searching for that answer to solve all of your worries- it is non existent. Desperately hoping that your mind will clear and wash your grief away in its melancholy river that never fails to trouble you.

Constantly. Waiting. Waiting. For something to happen, a change, a comfort- but that something never comes, for we grow old with our sadness and our loss, these are the things that make us unique and whole.

Rejection

Never mind, you will always have another chance, another shot, another go at fulfilling your dreams-for your destiny awaits.
However, when these other chances fail, what do you do? Do you give up, just like that? Or do you reflect back on it and try harder?
Enhance your mind, focus clearly, choose what is best for you, and understand that harsh rejection is part of the process that makes up your life.

Success

Jubilation resounding through your veins, pleasing your soul, and giving you extreme happiness and joy.
The intense feelings of being elated and successful can really aid in your reflection of your life.
Have you achieved what you wanted to? Have you made your loved ones proud? Enjoy the moment and carry on being successful, for your good spirit yearns for the celebrations of success!

Emotions

Emotions-the very essence that defines your personality, allowing your feelings to be transparent to the other people around you.
Emotions-the perfect way to express yourself.
Emotions-your life.
Emotions-you.

Time

The constant chime of the hour, the
relentless ticking of the second, the
measure of a life well spent.
Time.
Time is a constant reminder that
life here on earth is not infinite, and
that we have to carefully carve out
of lives, and shape our futures, in
order to live happily, and improve
the lives of the future generations
to come.
Time passes everyday and before
you know it-ah, it's the end of the
day!
So use your time wisely, make a
difference, and live your life to the
fullest!

Motivation

What is that vital thing that
encourages me to do what I do?
What helps me focus on the task
at hand?
Motivation.
Motivation drives you forward.
It is the backbone that holds
strong, dominant and superior,
pioneering your actions and
decisions in life.
It has the power to change your
mind and think differently.
Motivation.
The key tool to work harder and
shape brighter futures.

Potential

You have that special something
that everyone is talking about.
You have the ability to do great
things, and help other people.
You are capable of transform
people's lives forever.
You have potential.
However, you can only do these
things if you unlock your
potential, harness it and drive it
forwards.
Commandeer it in your
direction and live up to your
true potential!

Barriers

If you are diligent enough, you can achieve anything. The barriers to your achievements can be extremely annoying, but you have to overcome them in order to achieve anything. First, it is imperative that you focus and think carefully. Second, you must be calm and composed, for nothing comes from anger and frustration, you will only reap the rewards of success with tranquility and composure.

PTSD

Flowing back uncontrollably, the horrifying memories continued to give his mind a potent dose of emotional torment.

No matter how hard he tried, he simply could not rid his mind of his traumatic memories.

His whole life was affected by this.

At night, is nightmares kept him awake.

Day, the motions of day to day life reminded him of the horrors that he had witnessed.

They were permanent. They were consuming his mind and soul…

Technology

Need to research something?
Need to communicate with other people?
The answer is simple-technology.
Technology holds the abundance of answers, solutions and communication systems that we rely on during a day to day basis.
Technology can prompt us to carry out tasks and fulfill our duties.
Technology can aid in providing information for medical treatments.
Technology is important.
Technology is helpful.
Technology is life saving.

Dark

Swirling around in the deep
dark abyss of nothingness,
the solitude grew.
Paving its way towards the
endless depth of ashes, the
solitude strode.
Consuming all in its path, the
solitude ran.
Annihilating everything
around it, the solitude
catapulted up high, launching
itself into the strands of light
that it most desperately
wanted to put out-it failed.
The light prevailed.

Music

The sweet sound of melody
and harmony resounding
thoroughly throughout the
brilliant acoustic stilled the
soul and pleased the mind.
The effortless Mannheim
roller constantly resounding
in your head provided a sense
of rhythm   and structure.
Music has the power to lift up
our spirits.
Music can relax us.
Music can entertain us.
Music is the culmination of
our lives.
Music is everything.

Happiness

Happiness is that warm feeling that overwhelms us when we experience enjoyment and pleasure. Happiness can also provide us with a sense of comfort and relief as well. Happiness is the sole reason why we strive to live to the fullest every day. Happiness is the key to enjoying life-so preserve it, enjoy it, and attempt to experience it as often as you can!

Failure

The voices echoing in your head,
preventing you from going to bed.
How?
Why?
What?
How could you fail?
Why did you fail?
What did you fail?
These questions really put you
down, and stop you from trying
things that you think you might fail
and not be particularly good at.
Well, reflect back on these
questions, realise how and where
you went wrong, and perfect your
art.
Try again. Persevere.
Work hard.
Succeed.

Life

Life.
Life is an adventure.
Life is a journey.
Life.
Just hearing the word
reminds you that everyone
experiences this in the
world.
Life.
It is the sole reason why all
of us are here in the world.
Life.

Hope

Hope.
The single word that can change
our entire lives.
It can spark life, and encourage
us to carry on and persevere.
When all hope is lost, we
wander ourselves astray, yet in
the charming presence of a
glimmer of hope, the bulwarks
are not completely abashed, the
sea not overflowing, the
windows not shattered- but all is
calm, serene and bountiful.
The right way is still at hand,
the chance is still there.

Fury

The clenching of the fists, sharp
may they turn, swift in their
elegance, painful in their punch.
The sudden build up of constant
rage, fuming inside of the burning
fire within the torn soul-
all good is lost.
Suddenly, the temper sways and
fumbles, yet still remains a threat
and it still drives on yet attempting
to perform its blow.
One mighty punch, one swift strike,
one violent bash.
The fury is rife and uncontrollable-
it destroys the soul…

<u>Acknowledgements</u>

Thank you very much for making it this far, and reading my book!
It has been an absolute pleasure writing this, and I do hope that it has inspired you to write your own books, poems, or even just to read more. Thank you very much Amazon, for publishing this book for me. Thank you to my brother Mark for inspiring me to write this book, after he published his first book,(A Collection of Poems). Thank you to my family for supporting me along the way. Finally, I hope that I enlightened your mind!

George Majcherczyk-Olczak

Printed in Great Britain
by Amazon

46543698R00030